EQUALITY & DIVERSITY

by

Charlie Ogden

©2017
Book Life
King's Lynn
Norfolk PE30 4LS

Written by:
Charlie Ogden

Edited by:
Grace Jones

Designed by:
Drue Rintoul

ISBN: 978-1-78637-117-1

Photocredits
Abbreviations: l-left, r-right, b-bottom, t-top, c-centre, m-middle.

Front Cover t - OlegD. Front Cover b - Atomazul. 2 - Rawpixel.com. 4 - Morenovel. 5 - wavebreakmedia. 6 - Rawpixel.com. 7 - g-stockstudio. 8 - Rawpixel.com. 9 - AJP. 10 - StockLite. 11t - jbor. 11b - Tumar. 12t - anucha maneechote. 12b - Skyward Kick Productions. 13 - CRSHELARE. 14tl - michal812. 14m - Iessia Pierdomenico. 15 - r.nagy. 16t - f11photo. 16b - Jorg Hackemann. 17r - Stuart Monk. 18tl - Tim Ridgers. 18b - Aleksandar Todorovic. 19 - evantravels. 20 - oneinchpunch. 21 - Zurijeta. 22 - iofoto. 23 - michaeljung. 24 - Everett Historical. 25 - OPOLJA. 26 - Anchiy. 27 - Phovoir. 28 - Rawpixel.com. 29t - Pressmaster. 29b - Monkey Business Images.
Images are courtesy of Shutterstock.com, unless stated otherwise. With thanks to Getty Images, Thinkstock Photo and iStockphoto.

CONTENTS

Words in **bold** can be found in the glossary on page 31.

WHAT IS EQUALITY?

People in the world are not all treated the same. There are places in the world where people are paid less for doing the same job as other people, where people can't practise their own religion freely and where two people who have committed an identical crime won't go to prison for the same amount of time. You might think that these sort of problems only happen in other countries, but that's not true. There is **discrimination** like this in every country around the world.

A truly equal **society** is one where everyone is treated and valued the same despite differences in their race, culture, sex, age, **wealth** or religion.

THE OPPOSITE OF EQUALITY IS INEQUALITY.

This man is Sikh, which means that he follows the religion of Sikhism. There are places in the world where he could face discrimination because of the religion he follows.

It can be difficult to fully describe what equality means. However, there are three main areas where equality is usually seen as most important. They are:

Rights – these are things that everyone should be allowed to do if they want to. They include things like being able to vote, speak freely and own property.

Opportunities – these are the chances that people have to do certain things, such as getting an education and getting a job.

Status – this concerns how people are viewed in society. Everyone in a society should be considered to be equal to everyone else – no person should be viewed as better or worse than another person simply because of their race, sex, religion, age or wealth.

There are places in the world where not everyone has the same opportunities to receive an education.

SINCE 2000, THE NUMBER OF PRIMARY SCHOOL CHILDREN IN PARTS OF AFRICA HAS INCREASED BY OVER 20 MILLION. THIS SHOWS THAT MORE CHILDREN IN AFRICA ARE GETTING THE OPPORTUNITY TO GO TO SCHOOL.

WHY IS EQUALITY IMPORTANT?

It is important for everyone to be treated equally so that individual people feel at home in their community and so that communities in general become friendlier and fairer places to live.

It is important to accept everyone despite their differences so that we can live in equal and happy communities.

It is still common for people all over the world to be treated differently because of things about them that are out of their control, such as their race or sex. People who are discriminated against for these reasons can feel separated from their community and ashamed of who they are. Equality is about ignoring the differences between people and instead making everyone feel accepted and at home in their communities.

An equal society is one where everyone has the opportunity to get any job regardless of their age, sex or **background**.

Equality is one of the main factors that helps a society to become fairer. A fair society is, amongst other things, a society where all children are able to get a good standard of education, where everyone can make enough money to have a good standard of living and where any person can get any job as long as they work hard enough for it. A fair society is one where everyone is given the same basic opportunities, meaning that everyone has the same chances to achieve success. The world is not yet a fair society and people all over the world are discriminated against every single day. Some people have lived their entire lives being treated worse than others for **arbitrary** reasons. Equality is the first step towards making a society where these things don't happen and where everyone has the same chance at living a happy and successful life.

WHAT IS DIVERSITY?

Diversity simply means 'a range of different things'. However, when diversity is talked about alongside equality it takes on a new meaning.

While equality is about treating everyone the same and ignoring certain differences between people, diversity is about recognising and celebrating these differences. For example, employers should not focus on someone's religion, culture or sex when they are deciding whether someone should get a job. Decisions like this should be made based on how good someone would be at that job. However, completely ignoring these things about a person all of the time can make them feel like they have lost their **identity**.

Equality and diversity are both concerned with the differences between people. Equality is about understanding when these differences aren't important. Diversity is about understanding when these differences are important.

Diversity can relate to a lot of different things; however, it is most commonly used to talk about the differences between people's cultures. A person's culture is the **customs** and ideas that they are used to and it can often involve such things as the food they eat, the festivals they celebrate, the language they speak and the way that they act. The culture a person belongs to will often come from the country or town where they grew up.

DIVERSITY IS ABOUT RECOGNISING THE IMPORTANCE OF DIFFERENT CULTURES IN SOCIETY AND PROTECTING A PERSON'S RIGHT TO HOLD ON TO THEIR CULTURE.

This is the Holi festival, which is celebrated by Hindus. Festivals can be a very important part of a person's culture and religion.

A person's culture is often very important to them, especially if they no longer live around lots of other people who belong to the same culture. It can remind people of who they are, where they have come from and what is important to them.

9

WHY IS DIVERSITY IMPORTANT?

Diversity is important both for large societies and for smaller communities like businesses and schools. An organisation, such as a school or business, is diverse if it recognises and values the differences people have. People with different backgrounds, attitudes and experiences often have unique skills and original ideas about how best to do things.

Diverse organisations understand how useful people from different backgrounds are in making their businesses the best they can be. Everyone is shaped by their background and the culture that they grew up in, so one of the best ways to make sure that an organisation is able to do a lot of different things is to hire a diverse range of people.

Diversity in businesses can help to make them more successful.

Having a diverse society is important because it can open people up to new things that they wouldn't have had the opportunity to experience otherwise.

When societies become more diverse and people from a range of backgrounds begin to move into a society, aspects of all of their different cultures can become part of that society. New shops might appear on the streets, restaurants serving different types of food might open and different music might be played. All of these things make a society more exciting! Diversity makes life more interesting, helps us to understand and accept people for who they are and shows us how to be happy and open with the things that set us apart from other people.

Diversity can help communities to become more interesting and exciting places.

RACISM

Racism occurs when people are treated unfairly because of their culture, background, skin colour or **nationality**. It is one of the most common ways that equality between people is **undermined**. There is racism and **racial** inequality in every country in the world and people from every culture and background can be racist.

WHEN THERE IS RACISM IN GOVERNMENT ORGANISATIONS LIKE THE POLICE, IT IS KNOWN AS 'INSTITUTIONAL RACISM'.

In some cases, people are racist without meaning to be. This is often because a person doesn't understand another person's culture or how important their culture is to them.

In lots of countries, racism is so common that even police officers are known to discriminate against someone from a certain country or background. In the US, if a black man and a white man are accused of the same crime, the black man is six times more likely to go to prison than the white man.

Racism is still extremely common in government organisations all over the world.

Racism can make people feel bad about who they are and not accepted by their society. Unfortunately, however, racism can often be more extreme than this. There are communities in the world that almost completely lack any diversity. Sometimes the people who live in these places are all from the same background and don't often do things that are outside of their own culture. People from these places can sometimes be very aggressive towards people from other cultures. This is often because they haven't had much experience with people from different backgrounds and so they are distrustful of them. In places like this, racism can be so widespread and aggressive that people can feel very scared. This shows how, in certain circumstances, a lack of diversity in a community can sometimes lead to a lack of equality in a community.

SOME COMMUNITIES ARE EXTREMELY ISOLATED, MEANING THAT THEY ARE VERY FAR AWAY FROM OTHER COMMUNITIES, WHICH CAN MAKE IT DIFFICULT FOR THEM TO EXPERIENCE DIVERSITY.

RACISM IN HISTORY

Some countries used to have strict laws that limited the equality between people of different races. One such country is South Africa.

South Africa

This is Nelson Mandela, the first black president of South Africa. He spent 27 years in prison for trying to promote equality in his country.

In 1948, a new government came into power in South Africa that introduced a system of **segregation**, known as apartheid. It stated that people could only live, work and go to school with people who were the same race as them. Apartheid became a system that heavily favoured white people, even though the majority of South Africa's population was black.

Black people were forced to live in poorer communities and could be thrown into prison for going into the areas where white people lived. The system came to an end in 1994 when Nelson Mandela was **elected** as president by the people of South Africa. Mandela removed the apartheid system and made a lot of positive changes in the country.

RACISM TODAY

Today, lots of countries have laws that help to stop discrimination against people that is based on arbitrary reasons. In the 1960s and 1970s, the UK government passed three separate laws that helped to promote equality for people of all races. These laws made it illegal for anyone to refuse **employment** or education to a person because of their race or culture. It also became illegal not to allow someone into a bar, restaurant, club or other public venue simply because of their race. These laws helped to establish the equality of opportunities and the equality of rights that exists between people of all cultures in the UK today.

THE POPULATION OF **ETHNIC MINORITIES** IN THE UK HAS MORE THAN DOUBLED SINCE 1991, SHOWING THAT THE COUNTRY IS BECOMING MORE RACIALLY DIVERSE.

These are the Houses of Parliament, where new laws are agreed upon in the UK.

CASE STUDY: RUBY BRIDGES

Before the 1950s, schools in the US were often segregated. However, in 1954 the **US Supreme Court** decided that schools couldn't be segregated as to do so didn't adhere to the **US Constitution**, which states that all people must be treated equally. Schools for black children before this time were given little money and their resources were extremely limited.

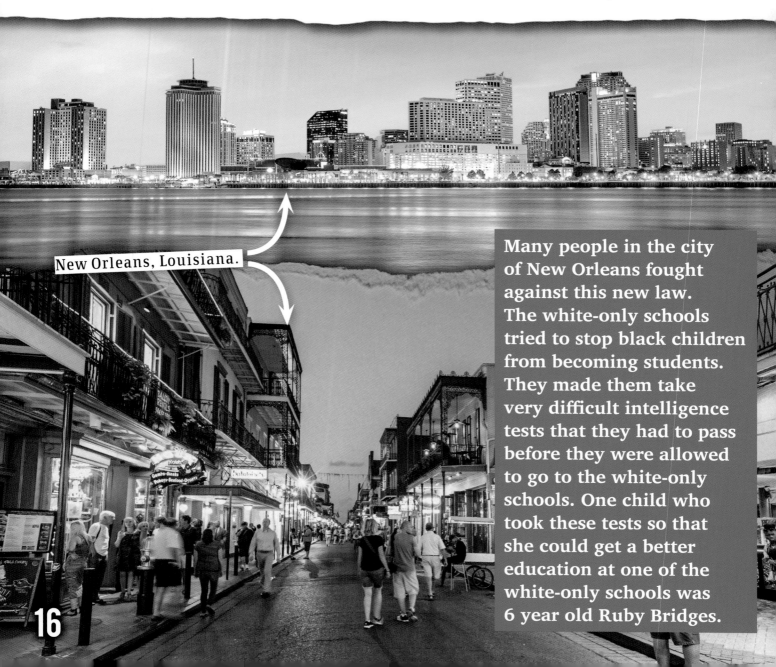

New Orleans, Louisiana.

Many people in the city of New Orleans fought against this new law. The white-only schools tried to stop black children from becoming students. They made them take very difficult intelligence tests that they had to pass before they were allowed to go to the white-only schools. One child who took these tests so that she could get a better education at one of the white-only schools was 6 year old Ruby Bridges.

Ruby was the only black child to get into William Frantz Elementary School and, for the first few weeks that she was there, she was discriminated against almost every single day. On her very first day, all the white students were taken out of the school by their parents.

They didn't want their children going to school with Ruby because she was black. Ruby had to deal with people shouting abuse at her almost every day as she walked to school. At times she was even scared for her life because people threatened to poison her food.

Ruby Bridges often had to be protected by US Marshals when she was leaving school.

Ruby stayed at William Frantz Elementary school until she graduated and she now runs the Ruby Bridges Foundation, an organisation that helps to promote the respect and appreciation of diversity. Ruby had to cope with a lot of discrimination when she was only a small girl, but in doing so she helped to make people of every race be seen as equal by society and she paved the way for a world that values equality and diversity.

RELIGIOUS DISCRIMINATION

Religious discrimination occurs when people who follow a certain religion, such as Judaism, Islam, Christianity or Hinduism, are not treated equally by other members of society. Many people around the world are discriminated against for the religion that they follow. People from every religion can be discriminated against and treated as if they aren't equal.

Often people will mistakenly discriminate against someone's religion because they are unaware of the religious beliefs of the people that they are with. People are sometimes unaware of the practices and rules that are part of a person's religion and they can accidentally be insensitive about them. It is important to understand and celebrate the diversity of religious beliefs in the world because it can help you to appreciate the lives of other people and avoid mistakenly insulting someone's religion.

THE MOST RELIGIOUSLY DIVERSE COUNTRY IN THE WORLD IS SINGAPORE.

This man is a Hindu. There are places in the world where he could be discriminated against for practising his religion.

STEREOTYPES

A lot of the religious discrimination in the world today comes from stereotypes, which are beliefs that people hold about other people because they are from a certain culture, country or religion. Stereotypes often concern certain types of behaviour that are expected of a person because they are from a certain culture, race or religion. Religious stereotypes are often formed in communities that do not have much religious diversity and are not accepting of different religions, which means that they are often untrue and hurtful.

Jewish people are often discriminated against through stereotyping.

Stereotypes are applied to all people from a certain culture, country, religion or race, which makes them a form of discrimination. This is because stereotypes group everybody with certain **characteristics** together without recognising their diversity or individual identities. Stereotypes, particularly hurtful ones, should always be avoided as they can be extremely harmful and do not recognise a person's individual identity, which may make them feel unaccepted within their community or society.

RELIGIOUS DISCRIMINATION TODAY

One religious group that is commonly discriminated against today is Muslims, who are people who follow the religion Islam. In recent years, extreme groups that claim to be fighting for Islam have violently attacked people for their religious beliefs and where they live. Most other Muslims do not agree with these groups and many of them have made efforts to try to stop these groups from hurting more people.

It is because these people are violent and they claim to be fighting for Islam that some people around the world have started to discriminate against all Muslims. This is unacceptable as only an extremely tiny number of Muslims, much fewer than one percent of them, are involved with these groups. This is religious discrimination as all Muslims are being discriminated against for the actions and beliefs of a very few.

MEMBERS OF THESE EXTREMELY VIOLENT GROUPS ARE KNOWN AS 'EXTREMISTS'.

While there is still religious discrimination in the world today, it seems as if people are becoming more accepting of different religions. In the UK in 2010, the government passed the Equality Act that specifically protected a person's right to hold any religious beliefs. The law also made it illegal for a person to be refused a job because of their religious beliefs. This law has helped to allow everyone in the UK access to equal opportunities and equal rights, regardless of their religion.

Nowadays, people from different religions often live and work together happily.

Laws similar to this have been passed by governments all over the world, which has made it so that many countries around the world are very religiously diverse. In particular, cities like London, New York and Paris have very religiously diverse populations that happily live and work together.

SEXISM

Sexism is a form of discrimination that targets someone based on whether they are male or female. Sexism often comes in the form of men not treating women equally and it has been one of the most common forms of discrimination throughout history. Sexism still occurs in every country in the world, making it one of the most important forms of discrimination to overcome in order to allow for an equal and fair society.

IN THE UK, WOMEN ARE SOMETIMES PAID BETWEEN 10% AND 25% LESS THAN MEN FOR DOING EXACTLY THE SAME JOB.

Today, sexism can often be found in the **workplace**. In many countries it is very common to see women working alongside men in all kinds of work. However, just because women may have access to the same jobs as men, it doesn't mean that they are treated equally to them.

Sexism can sometimes come in very extreme forms. Some countries around the world have strict laws that only affect women. These can make it so that the women in these countries don't get equal opportunities to men, don't have equal rights to men and don't have an equal status with men.

It is very common for women in Saudi Arabia not to be treated equally to men.

In Saudi Arabia, every woman must have a male **guardian**, which is usually their father or husband. Women are not allowed to travel, be involved in business, open a bank account or have certain medical treatments without the permission of their guardian. Women have very little freedom in Saudi Arabia and are viewed as less important than men by society. This can make it very difficult for women in Saudi Arabia to lead happy and successful lives.

SEXISM IN HISTORY

For a long time, women in the UK did not have suffrage, which means that they didn't have the right to vote in elections. However, in 1903, a woman named Emmeline Pankhurst and her daughters began a group known as the Suffragette Movement. Emmeline was not happy with the inequality between men and women and wanted women to be able to vote. The Suffragette Movement used many different methods to gain attention, including protests and even hunger strikes. These events made the UK government and people around the world notice the inequality between men and women and eventually, in 1918, women over the age of 30 were allowed to vote.

Three Suffragettes in New York, 1912.

Since then a lot of progress has been made in the UK to make women equal to men in **politics**. In 1979, the UK elected Margaret Thatcher as their first female prime minister.

SEXISM TODAY

While there still isn't perfect equality between men and women anywhere in the world, many countries have laws that help men and women to be treated equally. The first law of this kind to be put in place in the UK was called the Sex Discrimination Act and, in 1975, it made it so that a person could not be refused a job or an education just because they were a woman. Since then, many more laws have been passed all over the world that give women the right to be a part of government, to practise any religion they want and to work in a range of jobs.

Despite the progress that has been made, sexism still exists in every society in the world and so it is important that everyone makes an effort to reduce the inequality between men and women.

OTHER TYPES OF DISCRIMINATION

There are many other forms of inequality that are also widespread in societies around the world.

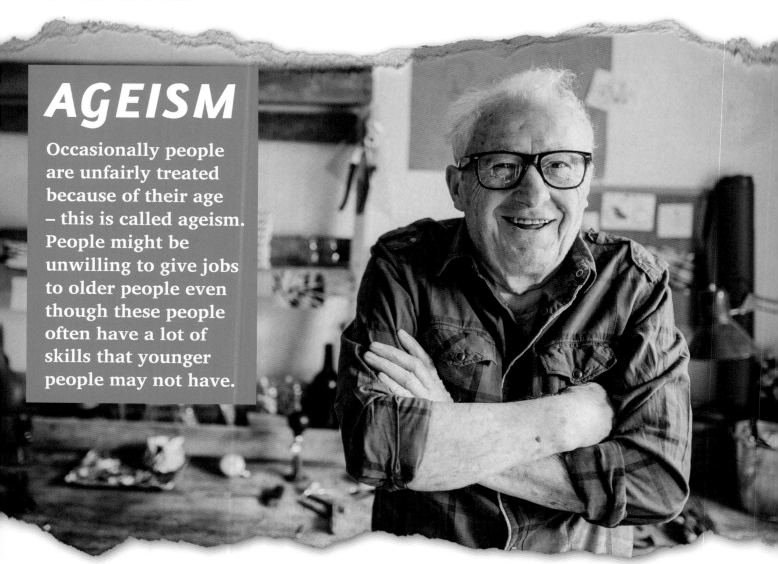

AGEISM

Occasionally people are unfairly treated because of their age – this is called ageism. People might be unwilling to give jobs to older people even though these people often have a lot of skills that younger people may not have.

There have been numerous laws put in place by governments around the world that prevent people from not employing a person because of their age. Despite this, people all over the world are discriminated against for their age, which can have an impact on their confidence, happiness and quality of life. It is up to everyone to treat people equally despite their age so that we can live in an equal and fair society.

DISCRIMINATION AGAINST THE DISABLED

Many people around the world have some form of disability. A disability is a mental or physical condition that a person has for their entire life, for example being **paralysed** and needing to use wheelchair. Disabilities can have a huge impact on the way people live their day-to-day lives. Being discriminated against for being disabled can make living a happy life very challenging for people with disabilities.

As with ageism, there are many laws that stop people from discriminating against people with disabilities. However, many disabled people still feel rejected and as though they don't have an equal status in society. It is important to make sure that everyone treats disabled people fairly and with respect so that they feel welcome and happy in their communities.

ONE IN EIGHT PEOPLE WORKING IN THE UK HAVE A DISABILITY.

People can be discriminated against for having a disability, which can make them feel rejected by society.

27

THE FUTURE

Over the past 100 years there have been many laws and changes in opinion that have helped to make communities around the world more equal and more diverse. However, there is still a lot of progress that needs to be made before we can say that everyone in the world has equal opportunities, equal rights and an equal status.

One of the best ways to help make the world a fairer and more equal place is by encouraging diversity in our communities, businesses and schools. By engaging with people from different cultures, countries and religions we can begin to learn how to forget our differences and accept people for who they are.

If the world is going to become a truly equal and diverse place, then it is down to every single one of us to help. There are many ways that you can help to make your school and community a fairer and more equal place. You can:

- Welcome everybody into your school and community.
- Show everyone respect and kindness.
- Not judge people on where they are from or who they are.
- Learn more about the different cultures and religions that are present in your school and community.

If we all try our best to encourage equality and celebrate diversity, we can make the world a better place for everyone.

It is up to everyone to try to make the world more diverse and equal.

ACTIVITIES

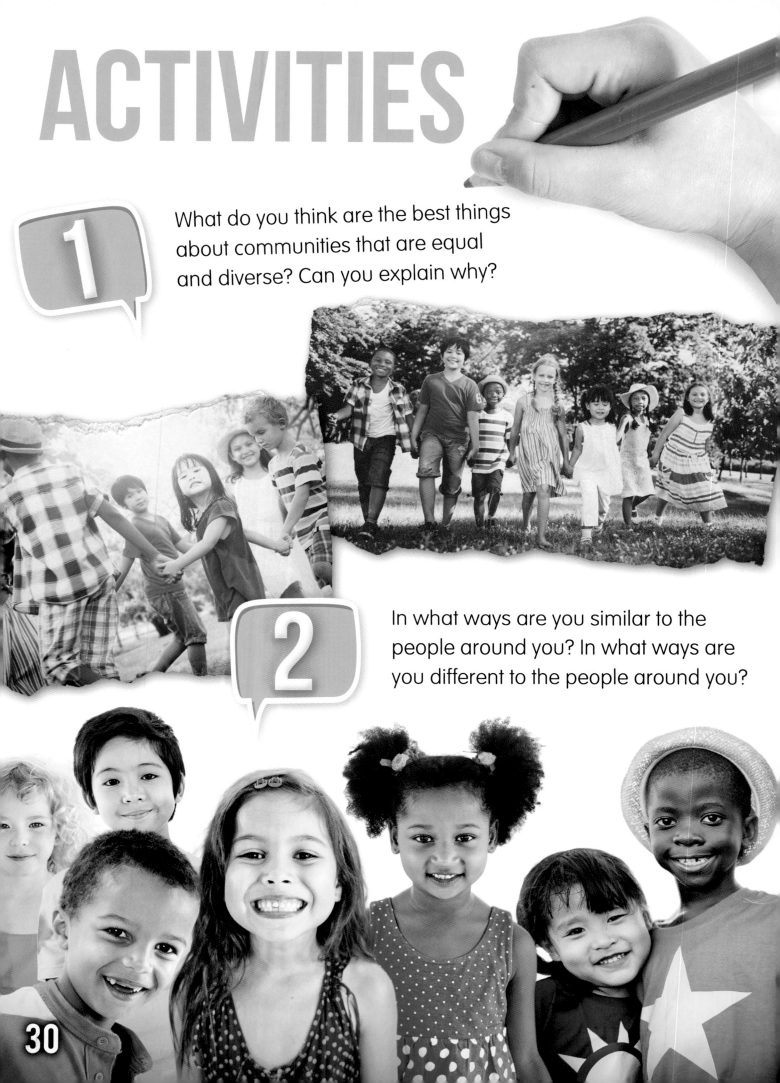

1 What do you think are the best things about communities that are equal and diverse? Can you explain why?

2 In what ways are you similar to the people around you? In what ways are you different to the people around you?

GLOSSARY

arbitrary	not based on any reason or system
background	a person's past experiences and social circumstances
characteristics	features of people that help to identify them
customs	traditional ways of doing things that are specific to a certain culture
discrimination	the unjust treatment of people based on arbitrary reasons
elected	voted for by the public
employment	the state of having paid work
ethnic minorities	groups that have different national or cultural traditions from the main population
guardian	a person who protects or owns something
identity	a person's view of who they are
nationality	the country that a person is from
paralysed	being unable to move part or all of your body
politics	the activities associated with the government of a country
racial	something that is related to race
segregation	the action of separating groups of people
society	a large group of people living together in ordered communities
undermined	something whose power has been lessened or weakened
US Constitution	the document that says how the US government should run their country
US Supreme Court	the people who make sure that the US government follow the US Constitution
wealth	the amount of money that someone has
workplace	a general term for places where people work

INDEX